*Born to have
a Special Companion...
your Pet*

Author's note:

Coming to America as a child holocaust survivor in 1948 with hundreds of other kids on the Queen Mary, I looked upward at my Papa and he smiled and said "Esty, mine kint, my child you are safe, you are in America. All is good.

Well, for me, yes I was grateful, did my prayers and thanked God I now had yummie ice cream, a warm clean bed and could look out the window and see the sun, and Papa didn't pull me away from the window...yes, Papa, all is good.

I started school - it wasn't so good, as Papa said...as I was teased, bullied. I looked different, acted different and spoke differently, dressed with oversized hand me downs and especially my hairdo. And I didn't have a Dog. I was just a kid, you know, and it seemed to me a Dog played an important part of fitting in America. I just wished to be part of America, to fit in, so I begged my Papa to get a Dog. We found one and I named it Blackie. Blackie became my everything, until Samantha found me...

Your Dog and Cat have that 6th sense and some have, I feel, a 7th sense. They are reincarnated, like old souls to come back to remind us to become more aware and bring us back to our true pure selves, and be of service. Meditate with your Dog and Cat and where ever you are emotionally, mentally and physically, you will be surprisingly brought back to what's most important in this life...

Partial proceeds from the sales of this book will be donated to Dog and Cat rescue causes. —e

First edition

Library of Congress
ISBN 978-0-9987395-2-6

Published by Estherleon Schwartz

Contact: esterleon@estherleon.com
www.estherleon.com

Illustrations by Ana J. Miro
Book and cover design and typesetting by Michael Rosen

Also by Estherleon Schwartz:
Tears of Stone and My Deal With God
Simply Meditate
Simply Meditate with Giggles

Distributed by Ingram
Printed in the United States of America

*Dedicated to the Miracle
and Joy of Animals*

~

Yay! We're back.

Believe it or not, mental telepathy, coupled with smell and physical gestures, may be your pet's 6th sense that kicks in to connect to your intuitive human sense...It's pure, trust it.

And...believe it or not, I feel that special dogs and humans have a 7th sense, like old souls. When we go to heaven, just maybe we are given a choice to be reincarnated as a dog or cat, for a special assignment: to bring about awareness and inspiration to our new human partners on earth.

Let's Meditate on gratefulness for each other to a Brand New Day, to live life with meaning and purpose and Love, especially to our new parent. Amen.

6am

Bow and Meow say to you...

"Thank goodness you're alive and awake. If only you could read my heart as I watched your breath as you slept. My love for you is beyond licks and a non stop waggly tail and Meow feels that, too."

It's the real deal.

Your pet feels all your emotions.
Through their 6th sense and that special
7th sense of pure intuitiveness, coupled
with reincarnation, they can help you in
so many ways, beyond the human touch
and scientific findings.

Simply meditate.
I lift my eyes and heart upward.
I inhale a deep, wondrous
breath of believing.
A calm surrounds me.
I exhale all doubts.
I swim in my calm.
I am grateful.
I am grateful.
I am grateful.

Mmm, yummy.
At last, real food.

7am

Breakfast grace with Bow and Meow
next to you, in silence:

I lift my eyes and heart upward.
I inhale a deep, wondrous
breath of pure life.

I inhale another deep, wondrous
breath of Divine gratitude.

A calm surrounds me.

Thoughts of love to each other
fill my being with more gratitude.

All is good. All is good. All is good.

8am

Bow and Meow are sending you a message:

Remember when you saw me and Meow among all the pets at the rescue kennel?

Teary eyed, Bow & Meow:
"It was love at first sight."

Simply Meditate...

Inhale a deep, deep wondrous
breath of pure life.
All is woof.
All is meow.
Folks, all is good.

Intuitively, you receive their tele-
pathic reminder to be mindful – an
awareness that brings back pureness
to your soul and refreshes your being.
It's an unexplainable process, or is it?

"I'm not a princess, I am a Queen.
I'm vegan and organic.
And P.S. thanks for leaving the TV on.
P.P.S. we love the Simpsons."

9am

Bow and Meow are sending you a message before you go to work.

"Could you bring home a special treat for us, the one we saw on TV? And Meow needs cat litter – the kind with the good smell. You know, Meow is very particular...Oh, well, she thinks she is a princess and runs the show."

Friends, it works.

10am

Meditation...

As Bow and Meow meditate at home, you may feel a calm, a presence surrounding you. Your pets see and sense what your soul could use some more of...that Divine calm.

Simply Meditate...

Lift your eyes and heart upward,
inhale a deep, deep Wondrous breath.
In this moment, an awareness of
gratefulness and joy surround you.
Never stop believing - have Faith.
One day, things will be different,
all in Divine time.

11am

You come home sometime during the day to check in and your pets greet you as if they haven't seen you in a hundred years. Makes up for any of the day's craziness, especially when your current job isn't the 'real' you. Your pets' greetings bring you back to a sense of joy, appreciation and love for those in your life.

Just
Be...

–Dani

12pm

A Simple Meditation for Grace at lunch

Suggestion:

Take a walk and, as they say, "Smell the roses." Sit on a bench, look upward, look around at all the beauty that surrounds you, as you are part of everything...everything is part of you.
Say grace before you eat that yummy nutritious lunch.

What a Blessing.
What a Blessing.
What a Blessing.

Hallelujah

1pm

Timeout...

When you and your pet meditate, you are connecting on a deeper, more spiritual level in the moment...those moments accumulate into more spiritual, magical moments of the body, mind and spirit.

"Meow. I just want to tell you
that I mucho love you."
"Arf, arf, me, too, love you."

2pm

" There is a place that beats
in my heart
in the shape of a tail and two ears.
With four legs, a wet nose,
and sounds of woofs and mews.
Filled with purrs and kisses –
hold every animal close.
For each one is our best friend,
A true companion until the very end. "

Authored by...Ajana & Pees

Right on.
Amen

3pm

Snack time:

A cookie a day – OK, OK, two or three, especially chocolate chip – brings on a 'high,' something unexpected, like a new, beautiful energy for the rest of the day – so appreciated.

Yay! Another amen

4pm

A mini Simple Meditation

Yes, with a little prayer here and there
around the clock.
Makes it thru the day; thank goodness no
emergencies; did have some fun on the run.
Daily challenges do come with moments of
Divine bliss out of nowhere. You know what I
mean, with that little prayer, here and there.

"Soon, we'll be done with our assignment and go back to heaven."

5pm

You...the chatter in your head:

"Gotta stop off at pet store and get a treat for Bow and Meow – gosh, so glad I remembered, just like that, it came to me. Hmmm."

"Friend...It's in the bag, it always was."

"I feel a surprise coming. I just feel it."
"Meow, meow. Me, too."

6pm

At pet store:

"Why not, yeah, get them this cute teddy bear, too? And this, too, and this, too. Everything in sight feels so right. So good to feel free to give."

"Giving is sometimes more than receiving."

When you believe,
all is possible
all is possible
all is possible
...e

7pm

"When you believe, no proof is necessary,
when you don't believe, no proof is possible."
– Stuart Chase

"Paws upward, Meow"
"OK, Bow"

8pm

"I hear the car. They're home. Yay. Let's act super surprised for all those extra, extra treats from the pet store," says Bow to Meow.

You...
"Sorry, Guys. Late din-din tonight! Gee, you two are always so...I can't explain it... Like, you're human?"
Meow says, "I think someone's starting to think out of the box."
"No puns, Meow. Let's say Grace."

"Yay, Hallelujah"

9-10pm

Everybody is on the couch watching disturbing world news. Bow starts barking and crying. You scratch it's head, as if to say, "What are you barking at?" Meow is meowing and meowing, I mean really meowing.

Bow says to Meow, "When we went to heaven as humans, we watched the world down there. We cried and volunteered and were chosen to be reincarnated as rescue animals. That was our assignment; to go back down to earth to help our new human partners that chose us. It was magical. When we looked into each others' eyes, it was like seeing, feeling each others' souls.

"Yeah, I remember how upset you were and I came over to you, you petted me and I knew I wanted to be next to you, to help."

"After this assignment is finished, we go back to heaven and do some heavy duty meditation and await our next assignment."

{your family
photo here}

11pm

"OK, guys, nite-nite time..."
You start meditating with Bow and Meow at
your bedside for all that is good in your life
and you're happy to have then cuddle next
to you. They jump up on the bed, everyone
cuddling.

Simply Meditate...a.k.a. evening prayer

We lift our eyes and hearts upward
and give a billion thanks
for this wonderful day of growth.
Moments accumulate,
giving clarity and power to your
newly refreshed thoughts
that turn into more wisdom,
gratitude and fulfillment.
This moment and every moment
is a Divine gift. Cherish it.

-e

12am

You're dozing off and seeing beautiful blue clouds in shapes of sheep, feeling a surge of strength, courage...you fall asleep.

Love Fur ever
...until...Fur ever

I couldn't make it without you.
I need your big loving eyes.
I need your enthusiasm
during my dark stormy skies.

- Your excitement when you see me like
you're always surprised.

I need your non-judgemental ways
I need you always on my side.

My rainy day pal when I just want to hide.

You know what you like
SO YOU CHOOSE ME

You're my friend and my confidant.
You set my heart free.
...With you Fur ever is where I want to be.

Authored by...Destiny

Iam

A noise wakes you up and you hear Bow snoring and Meow purring. They're in Nirvana. You go back to sleep, counting more of those cutie pie sheep.

2am

You have a dream. You're in heaven with lots of dogs and cats howling. You try to calm them down and meditate with them for calm.

I am Grateful

I am Grateful

I am Grateful

I am Grateful

3am

Still dreaming...calm now surrounds you.
You are feeling peaceful.

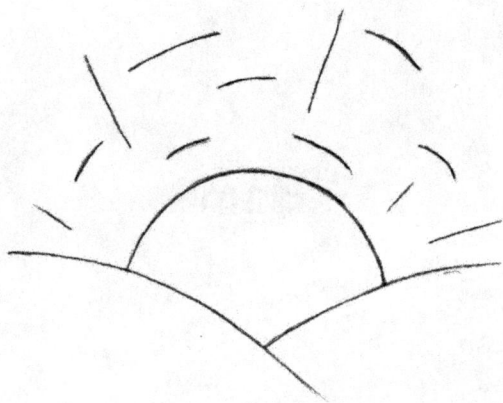

4am

You wake up slowly as you feel the
warmth of the sun rising.

It's a Brand new Moment
A Brand new Day

"We've finished our assignment.
Bye, bye for now.
Look upward with your eyes and heart.
You will feel a calm that surrounds you.
You can do it!
We love you," say Bow and Meow
Until we meet again.

5am

You wake up.

"I get it! That's it. I really get it.
I'm quitting my job. I want meaning and
purpose in my life. I think I want to rescue animals."

He looks for Bow and Meow.

They are gone.

He falls into a deep meditation.

P.S. "It's better to believe than not."

P.P.S. Simply Meditate, meditate,
meditate, meditate on

Clarity ~ Joy ~ Gratitude

I met Estherleon very much by chance, but it was totally meant to be. We clicked right away, kookiness and all, and got straight to work. We sat together, and after 2 hours of our imaginations working together and letting my pencil do its magic, we created the character of Bow and Meow. They were captivating, sweet and conveyed the emotions Estherleon was looking for. I finalized the images, had several other meetings to tweak all the images to perfection, and that is how, after being a visual artist my whole life, I illustrated my first book. And for that I will be always grateful to the universe for putting Estherleon in my path.

-Ana J. Miro
illustrator
www.anartistically.com

It was and is a soul felt, creative imaginative experience working with Ana. She gets it on the spot, draws it 1,2,3 - she is dependable and magical.

-Estherleon Schwartz

Upcoming book 4 of the series:

SIMPLY MEDITATE...
WITH ?

9 780998 739526